MW00625385

THE
SECRET
PLACE

Abiding Under the Shadow of the Almighty

ERIN JAMES SAIN

THE SECRET PLACE

Copyright © 2008 by Erin James Sain.
Printed in the United States of America.
All rights reserved.

ISBN: 978-1-886296-52-7

Published in the United States by
  Arrow Publications
  P.O. Box 10102
  Cedar Rapids, IA 52410
  Telephone: (319) 395-7833
  Toll Free: (877) 363-6889 (U.S. only)
  Fax: (319) 395-7353
  www.arrowbookstore.com

Unless otherwise indicated, all Scripture quotations are taken from the New American Standard Bible. Copyright © 1960, 1962, 1963, 1968, 1971, 1972, 1973, 1975, 1977 by The Lockman Foundation. Used by permission.

Scripture quotations marked "KJV" are from the King James Version of the Bible.

CONTENTS

FOREWORD

by Francis Frangipane

I have known Erin and Janel Sain for several years now. I must say, it has been a joy to watch them grow in Christ. They are passionate for the things of God and compassionate toward the people of God.

Erin is a fearless preacher of righteousness. For as long as I've known him, I cannot remember a time when he allowed the fear of man to dilute his message. When I listen to him preach or read his words, I'm aware that he isn't preaching from a sermon he found on the Internet; he's a man who hears from God. Indeed, this book is fruit and proof of Erin's own Secret Place relationship with the Lord. Each chapter is a lamppost lighting the way toward greater intimacy with Jesus.

INTRODUCTION

"He that dwelleth in the secret place of the most High shall abide under the shadow of the Almighty."

— *Psalm 91:1*

I wrote this book with the typical, everyday believer in mind. I feel I have something to share on the subject of fellowship with God. I am neither highly educated nor well versed in theological study. I simply know the Bible and have learned through experience how to apply God's Word to my everyday life. I maintained a focus on practicality while writing this book; I wanted to make it easy for the average believer to apply.

There are a lot of teachings available on this topic. This one is geared to be simple. Fellowship with the Lord is sometimes presented as complex and reserved for certain special people. But the Lord desires deep fellowship with *all* Christians.

I will share my testimony in this book because I believe it will help those of you who feel that true fellowship with God is unobtainable. We do not serve a distant, unapproachable God. We serve a God who invites us to *"come boldly unto the throne of grace, that we may obtain mercy, and find grace to help in time of need (Heb. 4:16, KJV)."*

THE SECRET PLACE

I believe that all Christians would like to have deeper fellowship with the Lord; most just don't know how. There are fundamental principles that lead to deeper closeness with Him. I will talk about how we can apply them on a daily basis.

Perhaps you have attempted to draw near to God and have run into barriers. I have been in that position; I remember hearing about other people's experiences with God and feeling that mine did not measure up. As I tried to draw near to the Lord, I sometimes felt I was going nowhere.

I have learned throughout my Christian walk that one of the worst things we can do is compare our experiences with others'. This normally leads to frustration. Many times we go into new situations with pre-drawn conclusions and false expectations that may lead to disappointment. It is important to remember that your relationship with the Lord is *personal*. It won't look exactly like mine or anyone else's. The Lord responds to us individually and differently as He chooses. It has a lot to do with our calling and gifting. He develops us uniquely to equip us for His purposes. We who have children in the natural do not respond to them all in the same manner. We have *personal* relationships with them. And these relationships are governed by many different factors, such as age, gender, and personality type. The same is true with the Father and His children.

But while each relationship with the Lord is unique, the principles by which we enter more deeply into the relationship are universal. There is a sort of "heavenly protocol" that is based upon the nature of God. This book will define these principles that we may all know Him in a deeper, more tangible way, coming to dwell in the Secret Place of the Most High.

Let's begin by reading Psalm 91, which describes the Secret Place and the rewards of dwelling there with God. Consider in your heart what it would mean for you to live this way.

Erin James Sain

*He that dwelleth in the secret place of the most High
shall abide under the shadow of the Almighty.*

*I will say of the Lord, He is my refuge and my fortress:
my God; in him will I trust.*

*Surely he shall deliver thee from the snare of the fowler,
and from the noisome pestilence.*

*He shall cover thee with his feathers, and under his wings
shalt thou trust: his truth shall be thy shield and buckler.*

*Thou shalt not be afraid for the terror by night;
nor for the arrow that flieth by day;*

*Nor for the pestilence that walketh in darkness;
nor for the destruction that wasteth at noonday.*

*A thousand shall fall at thy side, and ten thousand at thy right hand;
but it shall not come nigh thee.*

*Only with thine eyes shalt thou behold and see
the reward of the wicked.*

*Because thou hast made the Lord, which is my refuge,
even the most High, thy habitation;*

*There shall no evil befall thee,
neither shall any plague come nigh thy dwelling.*

*For he shall give his angels charge over thee,
to keep thee in all thy ways.*

*They shall bear thee up in their hands,
lest thou dash thy foot against a stone.*

*Thou shalt tread upon the lion and adder:
the young lion and the dragon shalt thou trample under feet.*

*Because he hath set his love upon me, therefore will I deliver him:
I will set him on high, because he hath known my name.*

*He shall call upon me, and I will answer him:
I will be with him in trouble; I will deliver him, and honour him.*

With long life will I satisfy him, and shew him my salvation (KJV).

CHAPTER 1:

RESTORING THE PRESENCE OF GOD

A shift was coming for Israel. King Saul's reign was coming to an end. Saul was the first king of Israel. He was God's chosen man. He had become king after the Holy Spirit came upon him, and he had prophesied with the prophets (1 Sam. 10:10). God blessed Saul with many victories. For a while, it seemed that He had everything going for him. The Bible says that he was taller and better looking than all the children of Israel (1 Sam. 9:2). He seemed to be royalty through and through. He had favor written all over him. It looked as if Saul had all the makings of a great leader… but looks can be deceiving.

During Saul's reign he strayed from the ways of God. He disobeyed the commandments God had given through the prophets, following his own desires. One important sign of Saul's self-centeredness is the fact that he neglected the ark of the covenant.

God had given Moses strict orders on how the ark of the covenant was to be constructed. It was to be constructed by a man named Bezaleel, which means "in the shadow of God." God chose Bezaleel and filled him with His Spirit. Bezaleel was specially gifted by God in works of metal, wood, and stone, and only he was qualified to complete such an intricate design (Ex. 31:1–5). It took a man with a name that means "in the shadow of God" to produce a work of art like the ark. The most fascinating thing is what God said after He gave Moses the specifications for the building of the ark.

And there I will meet with thee, and I will commune with thee from above the mercy seat, from between the two cherubims which are upon the ark of the testimony, of all things which I will give thee in commandment unto the children of Israel (Ex. 25:22, KJV).

So the ark was to be a meeting place between God and man. It was to be a place where Moses could hear the voice of God and "commune" with Him.

The ark also represented God's presence. Three items were kept inside as reminders of God's works. The first was manna, which God had caused to rain down as food for Israel while they were in the wilderness. This was a reminder of God's **provision.** The second was Aaron's rod, on which blossoms supernaturally appeared. This was a symbol of God's **power.** The third reminder was the tablets of the covenant. They were God's agreement with man and were reminders of God's **promises.** The ark is a prophetic picture of the reality of God's presence. There is great provision, power and promise for those who spend time in His presence.

But the Bible says that Israel did not inquire at the ark in the days of Saul (1 Chron. 13:3). As a result, Saul's house began to crumble. A man who had been the anointed, chosen king became depressed, insecure, and border line lunatic.

So Saul died for his trespass which he committed against the Lord, because of the word of the Lord which he did not keep; and also because he asked counsel of a medium, making inquiry of it, and did not inquire of the

Lord. Therefore He killed him and turned the kingdom to David the son of Jesse (1 Chron. 10:13–14).

Saul failed because he did not seek the Lord. His heart was so far from the Lord that he even went to a witch for answers.

One of the first things that David did after he took charge of Israel was to call a gathering of the entire nation to bring the ark of God back to Jerusalem. He organized a ceremony that seems to have been about as well planned as the opening ceremony of the Olympics. He hired singers, dancers, musicians and priests to accompany the ark. Then David led the way, playing and dancing before the Lord with all of his might. The entire nation was involved. When they arrived in Jerusalem with the ark, David addressed Israel with this psalm:

Give thanks unto the Lord, call upon his name, make known his deeds among the people. Sing unto him, sing psalms unto him, talk ye of all his wondrous works. Glory ye in his holy name: let the heart of them rejoice that seek the Lord. Seek the Lord and his strength, seek his face continually (1 Chron. 16:8–11, KJV).

David sealed his throne forever with this act. He led the nation back to God, back to seeking His face and away from the self-seeking reign of Saul.

I see this as a prophetic picture for today's church. God is bringing a shift. He is raising up a David-like people who will exchange the old, religious, self-serving agenda for true Spirit-led worship and service. I feel the heart of David: we must return to the presence of God; we must have only God leading our lives! There has been enough of the spiritless, dry, dead, fruitless type of Christianity. God is calling the church to wake up and return to intimacy with Him. That's why this book is for today. We must *inquire of Him* in His presence. We must be people who dwell in the Secret Place of the Most High.

CHAPTER 2:

ENTERING IN

The Secret Place of the Most High is where God dwells. In other words, it is His "presence." We should all seek to enter this place and find deeper intimacy with the Lord. The totality of our Christian experience is not getting born again. That is only the beginning. After we experience the new birth, we should long to go deeper. Sadly, many are content with a one-time "salvation experience" and seek very little to build upon it.

It is clear from Scripture that God talked and had fellowship with Adam. Adam and God knew each other well, and God was not some distant, far off, religious idea; He was Adam's Commander and Chief.

After the fall, a separation came between God and man. Some of that intimate fellowship was cut off for a time. Before Jesus saved us we were distant, even enemies of God, because of sin. The Bible says, *"The carnal mind is enmity against God"* (Rom. 8:7, KJV). But it is also written, *"Now in Christ Jesus ye who sometimes were far off are made nigh by the blood of Christ"* (Eph. 2:13, KJV).

Jesus saved us to reconcile us, to return us to right standing with God. Paul explained this in 2 Corinthians 5:17–18:

> *Therefore if any man be in Christ, he is a new creature: old things are passed away; behold, all things are become new. And all things are of God, who hath reconciled us to himself by Jesus Christ (KJV).*

God did not send His Son to die for us only to save us from hell. He sent Jesus to *reconcile* us. When you are saved or "reconciled" to God, you are brought back into right standing with Him. You become as innocent as Adam was in the garden before he sinned. You are repositioned to fellowship with God freely.

If we believe we have been forgiven and saved, we must also believe that we have been given all rights to fellowship with God. When we choose not to exercise these rights, we miss what Jesus' blood paved the way for.

Since we have been given this right, we must learn the heavenly protocol. Before an ambassador stands before a president or king, he must go through vigorous preparation. He must research the culture, customs, and protocol of the kingdom. An ambassador wouldn't dare to mosey into the presence of a king nonchalantly.

The pope recently visited the United States. I was amazed to see all of the preparations people went through to make sure that he was not in any way offended. Anyone who met with him was first briefed on the vigorous protocol for behavior in his presence. If men give other men this type of honor, how much more should we honor the Father by following heaven's protocol?

THE SECRET PLACE

GAINING ACCESS

The Bible tells us that Jesus is our only access to the Father. Jesus said, *"I am the way, the truth, and the life: no man cometh unto the Father, but by me"* *(John 14:6, KJV).*

We know that Jesus made a way for us to access God, but do we know what that really means? I think the modern American church has become numb to its meaning, partly because we have forgotten just how awesome God is. I am talking about the *Alpha and Omega*, the *Creator of all things*, the *Father of spirits*, the all-knowing, Consuming Fire—*God*. We have been given access to Almighty God through our Savior, Jesus Christ. This privilege, while staggering, is the true hope of God. In other words, it is not something that God has reserved for the elite; it is something He hopes for us all.

Proverbs 25:2 says, *"It is the glory of God to conceal a thing: but the honour of kings is to search out a matter"* *(KJV).* God's glory is in the concealing. Our honor is in the searching. We must pursue the glory and secrets of God with all our hearts.

Matthew 6:33 offers a key to understanding the protocol for entering God's presence. Jesus said, *"But seek ye first the kingdom of God, and his righteousness; and all these things shall be added unto you"* *(KJV).* Jesus was giving us the divine perspective: the best way to prioritize is always to *seek Him first*, placing God's agenda before our own. This is the most important principle to developing a personal relationship with God. We quote this verse in church often, but is it something we live? I will boldly say that until we put God **first**, we cannot experience the intimacy with Him that we desire. Many Christians and churches have it backwards; we are so busy seeking "all these things" that God has

> The best way to prioritize is always to *seek Him first,* placing God's agenda before our own.

taken a back seat. This mostly leads to frustration and failure. Upon closer examination, some who say that God is first in their lives might realize He doesn't even make their top three. We Christians must evaluate our lives. We must examine what we are pursuing. We must honestly gauge where the Lord fits into our list of priorities. How are we spending our time, money, and energy? I have talked with many professing Christians who say that they do not have time to read their Bible or have quiet time with the Lord; their lives are too busy. I think this is a senseless excuse for lukewarmness. I don't believe this will be a viable answer when we stand before the Lord one day to give an account of how we have spent our lives on earth. We can all make time to seek God if His kingdom and righteousness is our number one priority. This principle simply cannot be bypassed.

Think about the most anointed, blessed man or woman of God that you know. I am sure that a close examination of their priorities would prove that God's kingdom is first on the list. We would love to walk in the anointing, blessing and favor that they walk in, but we must first examine our own priorities.

There is a life of anointing, favor and blessing available to those who seek it. It is hidden in the Secret Place of the Most High, and the way is paved with the blood of Jesus. We can enter by properly prioritizing our lives—by seeking God first.

CHAPTER 3:

THE SECRET PLACE DEFINED

The Secret Place is a place only you and God know about. It is called "secret" because it is not something to be shared with others, at least not directly. It is a place where you meet God regularly, where you dwell daily. It is in the Secret Place that we should make all decisions. It is where we become the men and women God calls us to be. This secret place is established between you and the Lord, and in it you develop what I call a "God conscience." By this I mean you suddenly become aware that He is always with you, hearing your every word and seeing your every deed. Most Christians would probably agree that God sees and hears everything, but this goes beyond just consenting to that biblical fact. The God conscience is the awareness that you are being overshadowed by the Almighty. Psalm 91:1 says, *"He that dwelleth in the secret place of the most High shall abide under the shadow of the Almighty" (KJV)*.

Before developing this God conscience, you may have lived carelessly. Little thought may have gone into your ways. But now something is different. Every choice you make and thought you think is illuminated by the light of God's presence.

Suddenly, you are aware that the very hairs of your head are numbered (Matt. 10:30).

Everything changes; you walk in a new awareness of God that dictates your actions, attitudes, and choices. It is like having an invisible friend, only He's real and full of glory. Your heart begins to beat with the heart of God. You begin to realize that the way you used to live was unfruitful and vain. Your priorities begin to change and your vision comes into alignment with the kingdom of God. This happens as a result of God's work in you. You make the initial move to draw near to God, and then God responds by revealing Himself and His ways to you.

The Bible says, *"Draw near to God and He will draw near to you" (James 4:8)*. We often have it backwards. We say that we are waiting for God to reveal Himself to us so that we can get serious about our relationship with Him. But the Word teaches that God will not draw near to us until we draw near to Him.

This is not to be confused with the initial work of the Holy Spirit in you that brings salvation. I am not saying that you must prove yourself to God before He will save you. I am talking about closeness here. I am talking about becoming the friend

> The Word teaches that God will not draw near to us until we draw near to Him.

of God. I am talking about becoming sensitive to the Lord's voice; as Jesus said, *"My sheep hear My voice" (John 10:27)*. God moved upon you first to bring you to salvation, as discussed in my previous book, *Bearing Fruit that Remains*. The initial work of God drawing you to Jesus has nothing to do with your actions or attitude; it is the work of grace. But after He awakens you and reveals Christ to you, God looks for you to draw near to Him. The first work of grace puts us in position to draw near to God. However, many experience this work and decide not to go further.

THE SECRET PLACE

I want to talk to you about what happens when you have proven to God that you are sincere, when you have cultivated the faith that He gave you, and, suddenly, you attract God's attention. The Bible teaches that *"The eyes of the Lord move to and fro throughout the earth that He may strongly support those whose heart is completely His" (2 Chron. 16:9).* Think about this. God looks to show off in someone's life. He waits for your heart to become completely His. And then it happens—God begins to make Himself known to you. You begin to feel His presence with you; you develop a "God conscience." Suddenly, you no longer have to walk by faith in the invisible God. God becomes so real to you that you no longer have faith in the unseen; you have faith in what is known. Experiential faith. This is when Christianity becomes most exciting. You finally realize that you have been walking with God the whole time and that He has been working in you to bring you up into the realm of the Spirit. There your mind is washed in the blood of Jesus and you develop your "God conscience." This is what Romans 12:2 describes when it says, *"Be transformed by the renewing of your mind."*

> The moment we submit our life to Jesus and begin to follow Him, we enter the Secret Place of the Most High. It just takes time for us to recognize that we are there.

We may feel at this point that God has finally shown up, but the reality is that He has been with us the whole time; we have just finally become sensitive to Him. We have finally developed the awareness of the Secret Place of the Most High. This is not when you enter in; this is when you *realize* that you have already entered in. The moment we submit our life to Jesus and begin to follow Him, we enter the Secret Place of the Most High. It just takes time for us to recognize that we are there.

I remember going through this and feeling so detached from the world that it seemed I didn't belong here anymore. Sin became appalling to me. Everything that I did, heard, and saw was stringently evaluated in my spirit. I felt weird. I did not understand what I was going through. I know now that as I was seeking God and drawing near to Him, He was sanctifying me and changing me from the inside. Looking back, I realize that God was changing the way I looked at life and giving me His perspective.

I want to share a short testimony of my conversion because I believe it may help those who feel they struggle to find fellowship with God. I am writing this as a 29-year-old convicted felon who surrendered to Jesus in jail about six years ago. I submitted to God and, like many, I wanted to go beyond a one-time religious experience. I wanted this "personal relationship" I had heard people talking about.

In the beginning I did what I thought a Christian was supposed to do; I started reading the Bible. The jail preacher told me to ask God for a hunger for His Word, so I did. In fact, I asked Him over and over until it became the sincere cry of my heart, and then the hunger came. I began to read the Bible like I was starving and it was the only thing to eat; I read every day for hours on end. I got into the practice of sitting still for long periods of time, just absorbing God's Word. I would then write down whatever came to me.

After about seven or eight months of this, I knew the New Testament from front to back. I had developed a practice of sitting still just meditating on the Word; in fact my day was centered on it. I didn't know what I was doing; I was totally ignorant. But through this practice God was training me about the Secret Place.

The Scriptures made sense to me for the first time in my life. I had tried to read the Bible before and couldn't seem to grasp it. But now something was different. His Word became three dimensional, so powerful and full of life. I experienced Hebrews 4:12:

> *For the word of God is quick, and powerful, and sharper than any two-edged sword, piercing even to the dividing asunder of soul and spirit, and of the joints and marrow, and is a discerner of the thoughts and intents of the heart (KJV).*

I had no idea that the Lord was truly with me every time I opened the Word. I was unaware that the "ideas" that came to me were from God and would become the foundation for my whole Christian life and ministry. The Lord was there the entire time, teaching me and bringing the Word to life. I was walking with the Lord and did not even know it! Ignorantly, I was still waiting for God to show up and reveal Himself to me! I don't exactly know what I expected. Maybe I thought God would peel open the clouds or take me into the third heaven? My ignorance kept me looking for a supernatural encounter that would change everything in a split second. Wouldn't it have been nice if that was really the way it happened?

After my release from jail, I continued to walk with Jesus. My lifestyle was totally different. I did not act, talk, or even think the same. I was becoming a new creature. Yet still, believe it or not, I did not feel any closer to having fellowship with God.

About eighteen months later, I began studying some of Francis Frangipane's discipleship books, which had been given to me by the man who led me to the Lord. At that time I had a pressure cleaning business. One day I went to clean a roof, and the man who owned the home introduced himself as Francis. After I finished the job, he gave me a check and I drove away. After I had driven down the road, I looked at the check and saw that his last name was Frangipane.

I was shocked. Could this be the same Francis Frangipane whose books my faithful mentor had given me? I thought it was impossible since Francis lived in Iowa and this was Florida. But how many Francis Frangipanes could there be? I thought it was worth investigating, so I turned around and went back. I knocked on the door and when the man answered I asked, "Are you Francis Frangipane, the author?" He answered, "Yes, I am."

I was bewildered. His books were literally at my bedside at home and I had been reading them. I felt like someone was playing a joke on me. Someone was; it was God! Francis invited me inside, saying, "I can see this is a God thing." We stood in the kitchen talking about the Lord, and I made a connection that has changed my life greatly.

Shortly after that, my mentor, John, died at age seventy-eight. John's death was hard for me. He had been a true teacher and mentor. But God had known that this would happen, so He had brought me a new mentor and friend—in miracle fashion!

Having met Francis, I was excited, needless to say. I would go to his house to visit and ask questions about ministry and Christian life. One day I said, "I just do not feel like God ever talks to me." He looked at me and then down at my opened Bible and laughed. It was barely readable. I had underlined, cross-referenced, highlighted, circled and written thoughts on the empty spaces of almost every page! He motioned to the Bible and said, "If God is not speaking to you, then where did you get all that?"

Those words were a huge wake up call. I had been presumptuous enough to think that I had just thought it all up! I then realized that the countless pages I had written, my understanding of the Word, and the fact that I even had hunger for the Word were all due to God's fellowship with me.

THE SECRET PLACE

From that day on, I looked at fellowship with God in a whole new light. I realized that I had many misconceptions about the ways of God. I began to understand that God speaks through a number of sources such as His Word (the Bible), people, and circumstances, just to name a few. I had been waiting for the Lord to reveal Himself to me, unaware that He already had!

I thought back over the couple of years since my release from jail and recognized all of the ways that God had blessed me. He had been continually at work on my behalf. First, I was delivered from jail, avoiding the long term prison sentence that I deserved. When I was released, I had almost nothing. I was ten thousand dollars in debt with legal fees. I had no job, no car, my marriage was nearly dissolved, and I had to live with my parents. But immediately, the Lord began to open doors. I was delivered of drug addiction. My marriage was restored. My parents helped me buy an old truck. I started a pressure cleaning company from basically nothing, and within about one year, I was making great money.

The Lord favored everything I did. I was constantly blessed, both financially and spiritually. Despite all of this, I still was looking to start having fellowship with God; now *that* is ignorant! My life was being blessed because I had entered into the Secret Place of the Most High, and consequently I was being overshadowed by the Almighty. I was having fellowship with God and did not even know it. I felt like Jacob must have felt when he woke from his sleep and said, *"Surely the Lord is in this place, and I did not know it" (Gen. 28:16).*

I was like the men on the road to Emmaus who walked with Jesus after His resurrection. They walked and talked with Him for a good part of seventy miles without recognizing Him! They were actually followers of Christ, but Luke 24:16 says that *"their eyes were prevented from recognizing Him."* These two men had been devastated by the death of Jesus. They, like many, had expected Jesus to become the king of Israel and restore them to power. They had leaned on a pre-drawn conclusion of what Jesus would do, and they were now disappointed and frustrated by what seemed to be a failure. The Lord walked with these men and *"beginning with Moses and with all the prophets, He explained to them the things concerning Himself in all the Scriptures" (Luke 24:27).*

The Lord revealed to them that their expectations were incorrect, that the Scriptures clearly taught that the Messiah would suffer and die for the sin of the world. He opened up their understanding and cleared up their misconceptions. Then, later that night, Jesus took bread, blessed it and broke it, and their eyes were opened so that they recognized Him. Once their eyes were opened, Jesus vanished from their sight. Then those men looked back over the day and said, *"Were not our hearts burning within us while He was speaking to us on the road, while He was explaining the Scriptures to us?" (Luke 24:32)*

These men had walked with the risen Jesus all day and had even heard Him teach the Scriptures. Yet they were ignorant of His fellowship with them until the Lord opened their eyes. As I learned to walk with the Lord, I was ignorant that He was even there, yet my heart burned within me as He explained to me the Scriptures. Even after experiencing this for over two years, I still felt like God never spoke to me. I remember hearing testimonies of people who said God spoke to them in an audible voice. I wondered why God had never spoken to me that way. I thought God was keeping quiet with me, and it was simply frustrating. I have a feeling that many people feel like I did. We think we should be like others, and we begin to compare our experiences with theirs. This will always lead to frustration. Some may have extreme encounters in which God speaks audibly, but this is not the standard by which we should gauge our fellowship with Him.

THE SECRET PLACE

The next few years of my spiritual life flourished. I began to understand and cultivate this secret relationship with the Lord. I share this with you in the hope that you too will learn to abide in *the Secret Place of the Most High.*

Chapter 4:

Enemies of the Secret Place

Nothing brings me more pleasure than watching someone repent of their sin and come to Jesus. I have witnessed many people come to the Lord over the last few years. It is neat to watch as people come to God a mess and He begins to clean them up. There is usually excitement and joy initially, and then the moment of truth comes and they are challenged to persevere. Unfortunately, I have watched many give up. I want to discuss several of the hindrances that keep average people from reaching the ultimate goal for Christians—knowing and having fellowship with God.

The first is **misconception**. Most—if not all—people come to God with preconceived ideas and expectations about how He should respond to them. As you saw in my testimony, misconceptions about how God speaks and what it means to be close to Him can cause frustration. They can prevent us from realizing what the Secret Place really is and what it means that God has paved our way there.

I also believe that many people who have made the initial move of surrender and have entered into the Secret Place of

> The trouble is that many believers walk by sight. We go by what we feel or see and consequently live frustrated, confused, and unsure whether God even knows we exist.

God have ignorantly chosen later to walk away from it because it was not what they expected. God carefully watched over them as they fought to maintain faith and walk after Jesus; I believe that, in many cases, God painfully watched as they gave up in frustration because they felt God was distant. The Word of God shows us very clearly that God watches over, protects, provides for, and blesses those who follow His Son Jesus. Why can't we embrace this by faith? Does not the Word say that Christians are to walk by faith rather than sight? The trouble is that many new believers (and a lot of old ones too) walk by sight. We go by what we feel or see and consequently live frustrated, confused, and unsure whether God even knows we exist. This should not be! We must trust the Word and by faith believe that we are in right standing with God who is always there. Remember, *"Without faith it impossible to please Him"* (Heb. 11:6).

There is a period in which new believers must walk by faith in the Word without any experience. During this time we prove our sincerity and diligence. We must refuse to allow our circumstances to dictate our actions. We cannot allow emotions such as worry, doubt, fear, or confusion to defeat us or cause us to give up. We must learn to cultivate the Secret Place and develop intimacy with God—as *He* leads. We must guard against misconceptions that can rob us from knowing our God.

Disobedience to God's Word is another mighty hindrance to the Secret Place. When we walk in rebellion to the Lord's commands we must never expect to be close to Him. Our Lord Jesus said,

> *If ye love me, keep my commandments. And I will pray the Father, and he shall give you another Comforter, that he may abide with you forever; even the Spirit of truth; whom the world cannot receive... If a man love me, he will keep my words: and my Father will love him, and we will come unto him, and make our abode with him (John 14:15–17, 23, KJV).*

God has promised to respond to us when we make an effort to obey His Word. I have seen many new converts compromise their walk by refusing to obey, and they usually end up returning to their old life. It all starts with compromise, which leads to guilt, which turns into shame and ends up as condemnation. To avoid this cycle, one must take a bold stand on the side of obedience.

Another thing that keeps us from entering the Secret Place is **lukewarmness.** I want others to experience God in a deeper way, so I ask these questions: "Have you ever understood Christianity as a way of life?" "Did you ever start from scratch and decide that the Bible is worth reading and obeying?" and "What steps have you taken to make closeness with God a reality in your life?" We find God when we seek Him, as it says, "*Seek, and ye shall find*" (Matt. 7:7, KJV). Most people have never found God because they spend little or no time seeking Him. We will not find God by just going to church once or twice a week. (If you are looking for a quick-fix guide to intimacy with God, this book is not it!) We have access to God right now; however, in order to enter true fellowship with Him, we must make it a priority. It must become more important to us than television, games, work, hobbies, and even family. I am not saying we must give up these things, but they must take a backseat to seeking God's presence.

THE SECRET PLACE

Lukewarmness keeps us from closeness with God. Jesus adamantly opposed this intoxicating enemy in Revelation 3:15–16. He said,

> *I know thy works, that thou art neither cold nor hot: I would thou wast cold or hot. So then because thou art lukewarm, and neither cold nor hot, I will spew thee out of my mouth (KJV).*

I don't know about you, but I do not want to be spit out; I want to be brought near. The lukewarm want to be close to the Lord too—just not enough to do something about it. There is no fervency to move forward. Lukewarm people lack consistency. They make steps toward surrender and fellowship with God until something more interesting comes along. The lukewarm are easily diverted from the narrow path. The lukewarm lack stability and spend much of their time in the affairs of this world, concentrating their efforts on things which have little to do with God's kingdom. They want God, but on *their* terms. The problem for the lukewarm is that God operates on His terms, not ours.

> The problem for the lukewarm is that God operates on His terms, not ours.

This brings us to another enemy of the Secret Place: **the flesh.** 1 Corinthians 2:14 says,

> *But the natural man receiveth not the things of the Spirit of God: for they are foolishness unto him: neither can he know them, because they are spiritually discerned (KJV).*

God does not operate in the natural, fleshly realm; He operates in the Spirit. In order for us to have fellowship with Him, we must enter the Spirit realm. Jesus said, *"God is a Spirit:*

and they that worship him must worship him in spirit and in truth" (John 4:24, KJV). When we have fellowship with God, He does not come down to our level but brings us up to His.

This is why a person who is controlled by their flesh can never have true fellowship with God. Since *"they that are in the flesh cannot please God"* (Rom. 8:8, KJV), we must learn to be led and controlled by the Spirit. Fellowship with God requires the death of our fleshly desires. The Bible says, *"Now those who belong to Christ Jesus have crucified the flesh with its passions and desires"* (Gal. 5:24).

The flesh is lazy and does things halfheartedly. We in the body of Christ should never simply "mosey" into God's presence and ramble on with halfhearted prayers, the kind that we immediately forget about. We should come into His presence with a sober mind, with our heart fixed on Him. We should be as prepared to meet Him as we prepare to meet our most beloved friend or lover. We should meet Him with anticipation and singleness of heart. We should enter His presence with clear and concise thoughts.

Consider the way we issue earnest effort all day at our jobs and in our human relationships. It is an abomination to give our best effort to men and put forth little effort to cultivate our relationship with Jesus. We must become very serious about our relationship with Him. We cannot go on in the old way, being governed by the flesh.

We must come to the end of ourselves. This is tied to the principle we established in chapter one, *seek first the kingdom of God and His righteousness*. As we seek God, we must realize that He will not be taken out of His place in the Spirit. Our only hope of intimacy with Him is to lose sight of our lives in the natural, "flesh realm" and enter the place of the Spirit.

What is funny is that I did this almost by accident. As I learned the Word, I realized that Christianity required an entire life change, and I began conforming to what the Bible teaches. To me it was so simple; I just did what the Bible said. I struggled, of course, but I did not give up, and before long I had become a new person. I learned to walk in the Spirit by obeying the Word. Pretty soon my flesh (my natural self) was dying, and I was having fellowship with God.

If we want to experience fellowship with the Lord, we must be willing to deny our flesh. It is pertinent, and it is a requirement! I think that this is one of the biggest hang-ups for people in the church today. Too many just don't want to give up their old life and old ways, and consequently too many feel distanced from God. We must come to a place where we yield daily to the Spirit of God; this is the way into the presence of God.

Jesus said, *"No one can come to Me unless the Father who sent Me draws him" (John 6:44).* God will come to us in the natural realm to draw us to Jesus, but as He is drawing us to Jesus, He is drawing us into the Spirit. He is leading us to repentance and surrender; He is leading us to deny ourselves, take up the cross and follow Jesus (Matt. 16:24). When we make this move, we will begin to have fellowship with God—guaranteed! We may not realize it, we may not hear an audible voice, and we may not even feel different; but it is high time that we stop trusting our feelings and start believing His Word. This is why **unbelief** is also an enemy of the Secret Place. We must embrace our position with the Lord by faith; in time, the reality and awareness will come. We must not be those who draw back due to unbelief or doubt. I am encouraging you to press forward, believing

> We may not hear an audible voice, and we may not even feel different; but it is high time that we stop trusting our feelings and start believing His Word.

that God is for you and with you. All those who choose to deny themselves and make God their number one priority by daily reading and obeying the Word will develop intimacy with God in the Secret Place of the Most High.

For review, some enemies of the Secret Place as described in this chapter are misconception, disobedience, lukewarmness, the flesh, and unbelief. These are extreme foes which must be combated. This is what Peter meant when he warned us, *"Be sober, be vigilant; because your adversary the devil, as a roaring lion, walketh about, seeking whom he may devour"* (1 Pet. 5:8, KJV).

The devil does not have the power to just walk around devouring any Christian he wants to. This verse says that he seeks whom "he may" devour. In other words, he is looking for an opening in your life. He is looking for an area where you are not covered, an area where you are exposed by sin. It is there that he comes to devour. We can stand against such attacks by walking in submission to God. As the Word says, *"Submit yourselves therefore to God. Resist the devil, and he will flee from you"* (James 4:7, KJV).

CHAPTER 5:

GOD BENEFITS

"Bless the Lord, O my soul, and forget not all his benefits."

— *Psalm 103:2 (KJV)*

I have good news. There are benefits to serving God! You may struggle, fight, and war to draw near to Him. You may suffer pain, confusion, and hurt as you leave the *old you* behind. But when God draws near and accepts you as a son, the benefits outweigh the price by far!

Psalm 91 describes some of the many benefits of dwelling in the Secret Place of God. First, it teaches that when we dwell in the Secret Place of the Most High, we are **protected by God**.

This fact is clear throughout the psalm. Verse one says we will be overshadowed by the Almighty. In verse two, David calls God his refuge and fortress. These are military terms that describe a place of fortified protection. Specifically, a *refuge* is a place where you go to get away from danger, difficulty or hardship; it is a place of rest. A *fortress* is a military stronghold, a place of extreme safety. As we dwell in a secret relationship with God, we make Him our rest. He becomes our stronghold against danger. This is confirmed in verse 4, which says God will *"cover thee with his feathers, and under his wings shalt thou trust."* The psalm also says,

> *A thousand may fall at your side and ten thousand at your right hand, But it shall not approach you... No evil will befall you, nor will any plague come near your tent. For He will give His angels charge concerning you, to guard you in all your ways (Ps. 91:7, 10–11).*

These verses make it clear that the Secret Place is a place of divine protection.

It is comforting to know that we can depend on God to watch over us. These verses teach us that we have protection in several ways. First and most obvious is physical protection for our bodies. Secondly, we are promised protection for our "tent," which is our home. Verse 6 says that we don't have to worry about *"pestilence that stalks in darkness, or of the destruction that lays waste at noon."* In the threat of recession, this means something. I can personally say that this year (2008) has been my best year of business ever. Many of my peers have been forced to close their businesses and some have even had to move elsewhere to find work. I use zero advertisements except satisfied clients and word of mouth. The secret to my success is the Secret Place of the Most High!

Another benefit of dwelling in the Secret Place is **deliverance from evil**. Most of us have evil or sin that we want deliverance from. There are innumerable teachings available on the subject of deliverance. Some ministries focus solely on deliverance, and I believe a lot of these are beneficial to the body of Christ. However, I have a different approach to deliverance than some. I believe that when people develop a secret relationship with

THE SECRET PLACE

> I believe that when people develop a secret relationship with the Lord, deliverance is imminent.

the Lord, deliverance is imminent. People go here and go there to the next conference or book, looking for deliverance from some form of evil. It almost seems as if we've forgotten that the Lord can supernaturally deliver us from any and every evil, in an instant. Books and conferences are valuable, but developing intimacy with God is priceless!

Psalm 91:3 says, *"It is He who delivers you from the snare of the trapper."* God has supernaturally delivered me from many things. As I repented and made up my mind that I wanted to be free, things that had seemed almost impossible to give up became menial in the light of His presence. Huge struggles seemed to vanish as my walk with God progressed. I focused on some struggles, taking deliberate steps to be free. But others simply lost their hold as I walked with God. He was always faithful to show me when there was something I needed to confess or change. This should be normal for converts. This is the work of God in man, bringing freedom. As John 8:36 says, *"If the Son therefore shall make you free, ye shall be free indeed"* (KJV). Psalm 91:14–15 says,

> *Because he has loved Me, therefore I **will deliver him;** I will set him securely on high, because he has known My name. He will call upon me and I will answer him; I **will be with him in trouble; I will rescue him** and honor him.*

As we set our love upon God, He delivers us from sin. It may not happen overnight, but as we seek first the kingdom of God and His righteousness, we will see changes. Counseling couldn't fix it; self-help couldn't help it; but a secret relationship with God can destroy the evil that binds us!

There are many other benefits of dwelling with God. Maybe the most important to me is **peace in my heart**, a peace that says that no matter what happens, God is with me and will work everything out for my good. Romans 8:28 says, *"And we know that God causes all things to work together for good to those who love God, to those who are called according to His purpose."*

Before I walked with God, there was little peace in my heart. I usually felt anxious and out of place. I tried to find peace in many different ways, to no avail. If only I had known that lasting peace is found only in the Secret Place with God! We are like fish out of water apart from a relationship with the Lord. We were created to live in fellowship with Him. When we are not living in this fellowship, we are out of our element and can never find lasting peace.

The benefits of God are beyond compare. He cares for and loves His children. I try to help people understand an important principle from this verse:

> *Or do you not know that your body is a temple of the Holy Spirit who is in you, whom you have from God, and that you are not your own?* ***For you have been bought with a price*** *(1 Cor. 6:19–20).*

If we truly belong to God, if we have truly given Him all rights to the control of our life, then we are no longer "our own," *for we have been bought with a price.* Think about what this means. We were purchased by God. The price He paid for us was the blood of His own Son, Jesus. God owns us, assuming we have given Him ownership by accepting and submitting to Christ. If God owns us, then He is responsible to watch over us. Do you think God would fail to take care of His possessions? God has something invested in us; He has interest in us. He will be faithful to watch over His interests and maintain His possessions. We have no room to fret or worry about our life if we dwell in the Secret Place. God has obligated Himself by His Word to be our ever-present help in time of need. We serve a good God!

We can have confidence in the Secret Place. I am not talking about self-confidence; I am talking about confidence in God. The Bible says, "*Thou wilt keep him in perfect peace, whose mind is stayed on thee: because he trusteth in thee*" *(Isa. 26:3, KJV)*.

To understand all of the benefits of God, one must only understand God Himself. When we are connected to God we have access to all of His blessings and resources. God's resources are limitless, His power is immeasurable, and His hand is mighty to save. How then shall we be afraid?

"Blessed be the Lord, who daily loadeth us with benefits."

— Psalm 68:19, KJV

CHAPTER 6:

APPROVED IN SECRET

What does this *Secret Place* look like in practical day-to-day living? Jesus taught about this while on earth. In Matthew 6:1–18 He taught on three major issues:

— **Giving,** which includes finances as well as works and reaching out to others.

— **Prayer,** which is communication with God.

— **Fasting,** which is a form of worship and intensifies prayer.

*Beware of practicing your righteousness before men to be noticed by them; otherwise you have no reward with your Father who is in heaven. So when you give to the poor, do not sound a trumpet before you, as the hypocrites do in the synagogues and in the streets, **so that they may be honored by men.** Truly I say to you they have their reward in full (Matt. 6:1–2).*

Jesus started this passage by challenging our motives. The motive of the heart is perhaps the most important of all virtues. Why do you do what you do? I have found that we

> It's not medication we need; it's a *Secret Place* relationship with God. Medications mask the problem; God's presence will deliver you from the problem.

all live to please either God or people. A person who goes about making a big show of their good deeds proves that they do not have a secret relationship with the Lord. When we have a genuine relationship with the Lord, we care very little about man's approval and gratitude because we have the approval of our Heavenly Father.

We are created with a need for approval, and being raised with a lack of it can negatively affect the way we feel about ourselves and others. Just look at this "fatherless generation" that feels so unapproved, unaccepted, and rejected that they cut themselves and run to drugs, sexual immorality, and violence. If only we would realize that it is the approval of God that we really need. We must maintain a healthy relationship with the Lord in order to feel approved. When we neglect this, we feel unapproved and often act artificially to be noticed and receive approval from man. It should be our God conscience that causes us to act and talk. We should do everything to please God and win His approval. A person who knows God approves of them is mentally stable.

Today's culture makes a big deal about self esteem. I believe that true self esteem is the knowledge that God esteems you. The approval of God offsets the rejection of man. I believe people who "suffer" from low self esteem are really suffering from a lack of confidence in God's approval. How can you esteem yourself lowly if you know you have God's esteem? It's not medication we need; it's a *Secret Place* relationship with God. Medications mask the problem; God's presence will deliver you from the problem.

So Jesus was teaching us to live our lives as if God is the only one watching. It is a "secret"; no one needs to know that you gave money, volunteered at church, helped your neighbor, or did any other good deed. These are just things you do because of your relationship with God, and His approval is enough. Jesus even said,

> *But when you give to the poor, do not let your left hand know what your right hand is doing, so that your giving will be in **secret**; and your Father **who sees what is done in secret** will reward you (Matt. 6:3–4).*

There are rewards for those who live a secret life before God. These *rewards* or *benefits* are all the good things in life that we search for but can't seem to find. We will find these rewards commonplace in our lives if we follow Jesus' teaching to live in secret with God. Jesus also used this principle when teaching on prayer. He said,

> *When you pray, you are not to be like the hypocrites; for they love to stand and pray in the synagogues and on the street corners **so that they may be seen by men.** Truly I say to you, they have their reward in full. But when you pray, go into your inner room, close your door and pray to your Father **who is in secret,** and your Father **who sees what is done in secret** will reward you (Matt. 6:5–6).*

When we make a show of our prayers to be seen by man, we lose our reward from God. Prayer is communication with God and should be done in secret. Imagine being in a room full of people with your spouse by your side and talking loud enough that everyone can hear you. You would not do that. You probably would not want people to hear your private conversation. Your only concern would be speaking loud enough for your spouse to hear. I understand that there is a time for corporate prayer, just as there is a time for public conversation. But if your prayer life exists mostly in front of others, it may be artificial and geared to impress man rather than communicate with God. We must search out the motive of our hearts.

When teaching on fasting, Jesus said,

> *Whenever you fast, do not put on a gloomy face as the hypocrites do, for they neglect their appearance* **so that they will be noticed by men** *when they are fasting. Truly I say to you, they have their reward in full (Matt. 6:16).*

He was describing people who make a show of their fasting to be recognized by man and consequently lose their reward from God. What a waste of time! Is it worth starving yourself only to hear a man say, "You are doing a good thing"?

> *But you, when you fast, anoint your head and wash your face so that your fasting* **will not be noticed by men,** *but by your Father* **who is in secret;** *and your Father* **who sees what is done in secret** *will reward you (Matt. 6:17–18).*

It is clear from Jesus' teaching about giving, praying and fasting that God wants us to live a *secret* life with only Him. This is what a "personal" relationship is. It is interesting that Matthew 6 says that our Father *is in secret*. It sounds like God lives in this *Secret Place*. If we want to be with Him, we must go where He is. This takes a great leap of faith.

In order to enter this *Secret Place* where we stop caring whether we are noticed by man, we must have total faith that **God sees what is done in secret** and that **He will reward us.** The Word says that God will see us and promote us, with or without man's approval. I always carry Matthew 23:12

with me because it helps me keep this in perspective. It says, *"Whoever exalts himself shall be humbled; and whoever humbles himself shall be exalted."*

A person focused on living only to please God will not exalt himself or herself to be noticed by man. If you want to be advanced, to be used by God, to have a ministry—pay close attention. If you do things to prove that you are anointed or to be noticed by man, hoping to be promoted, you will be humbled. However, if you focus on your secret relationship with God, living like He is the only one you care about pleasing, God will exalt you; God will promote you because of your humility. This is a kingdom principle.

There are a lot of people in ministry who are not happy where they are; they are out of place and out of God's will. People quit ministry every day because of frustration, confusion, and stress. I believe the reason is often that they have promoted *themselves* into positions that God did not create them for. Instead of waiting on God to promote them, they settled for something less than His best. Don't let that happen to you. Believe that God purchased you, that He is responsible for you, and that He has a plan for you. Be patient, live pure, and wait for God to promote you in due season.

Joseph is a prime example of this (Gen. 37–41). He waited on God and was promoted from foreign prisoner to leader of one of the most powerful nations in the world. It was God who promoted Joseph; no man could have done it. He had a vision to be used by God. He was sold into slavery by his own brothers. He was falsely accused by a seductive woman. He had every opportunity to fail, harden his heart, and give up on the

> If you focus on your secret relationship with God, living like He is the only one you care about pleasing, God will exalt you.

promise of God, but he didn't. He persevered; he maintained his purity, patience, and confidence; and he overcame. God supernaturally exalted Joseph to rule because He could trust Joseph to remain faithful.

Are you willing to wait on God while you walk in humility, or will you promote and exalt yourself before your time? I hope you choose to wait on God. It may be more difficult and it may take longer, but when He promotes you, it will be permanent and it will be exactly the position you were created for.

CHAPTER 7:

DISCOVERING YOUR IDENTITY

The Secret Place is about living continually in the reality of God's presence. Acts 17:28 says, *"For in him we live, and move, and have our being" (KJV)*. The Secret Place encompasses your entire life in Him. However, I do want to focus specifically on the time of day when you lay everything else in your life to the side and focus solely on the Lord.

This is your one-on-one time with God. Some people call it their "quiet time." Every Christian should have a daily time when they turn off the television, computer, cell phone and all other distractions and focus only on the Lord. The purpose of this time is to discover your identity in the Lord, to find out why God created you.

I have personally ministered to hundreds of people, and I have realized something that troubles me. Not many Christians have any idea what their calling is, and most are not searching very hard to find out. They have no identity. It seems like many are just passing their time here on earth with little purpose or direction. It's as if we are just waiting to die. This should not be!

THE SECRET PLACE

The Bible clearly teaches that God had a plan for our lives before we were even created. Ephesians 1:4 says, *"He (God) chose us in Him (Christ)* **before the foundation of the world,** *that we would be holy and blameless before Him, in love."* It is beyond our comprehension that God *chose us* before He even created man. This truth is confirmed in Ephesians 2:10: *"For we are His workmanship, created in Christ Jesus unto good works, which God hath* **before ordained** *that we should walk in them" (KJV).* Our lives were *ordained* by God, *before the foundation of the world.* He has already mapped the course and set the stage for our success in Him. First Corinthians 7:7 says, *"Each man has his own gift from God."* Think about this. God has already decided what He wants to produce with our lives, and He gifted us to fulfill that purpose. He knows why we are here, even if we do not. As Christians, our sole focus should be to seek God's plan for our lives. It should be to find our identity in the Lord.

"Seek **first** *the kingdom of God..."* True life is really about finding our position in the kingdom of God. We will only find God's plan for our life as we seek it. We should spend time every day with God, seeking His will for our life and discovering our identity. In this time we will develop intimacy with God. There is no other way to grow closer to the Lord. Some believe that we will grow closer to God if we just do good deeds, but good works are no substitute for spending time with Him. Growing closer to Him is about dwelling in His presence. Intimacy with God is not something you will just wake up with one day. Intimacy with God is developed, not imparted. It is brought on by a lifestyle practice, not given as a gift. You must cultivate it through constant, daily decisions to set yourself apart and draw near to God.

CHAPTER 8:

FREEDOM TO BE YOU

It is important to understand that we are all different and that God relates to each of us as individuals. I am very cautious about "one size fits all" guidelines to anything. All Christians have different experiences and relationships with the Lord. I learned this mainly by comparing my relationship with God to my wife's relationship with God.

My wife's calling is that of an intercessor. All Christians are called to pray, but God has specially called her to pray specific things that He reveals to her. A lot of her time is spent in intercession for others. The Lord burdens her for people, countries, or problems in people's lives. He leads her to pray for deliverance, blessing, or help to those in need. She has a prayer wall covered with pictures of those whom she prays for, and she goes to battle for the ones the Lord leads her to pray for.

My gifts and calling are more for teaching, preaching, evangelism, and discipleship. My time with the Lord is usually spent in the Word and in long periods of meditation. I often sit for hours while the Lord brings His Word to life and I write down what He shows me. These revelations usually become sermons, teachings, or fuel for personal ministry.

Early in my ministry I expected everyone else to do what I did because it worked for me. I discovered later that God does with each person as He pleases according to their calling and His plan for their life. My wife's one-on-one time with the Lord is different than mine. Because there is a difference in our callings, there is a difference in our Secret Place. One of the worst things that we can do is to try to force our relationship with God onto someone else. We must allow God to develop this with each believer as He wills.

But with that in mind, there are some common principles that bring us all closer to the Lord. God does not change. He may relate to each of us differently, but His nature is constant. By understanding His nature, we can understand what He likes and doesn't like. If we want God to find pleasure in us, it is important to be wise in our pursuit of Him.

Reading the Word is one of the greatest ways we can all discover our destiny in the Lord. There is a real and persistent attack from the enemy to keep us distracted and to prevent us from reading the Bible because of the danger it inevitably brings to Satan's kingdom. I love Psalm 119:105, which says, *"Thy word is a lamp unto my feet, and a light unto my path" (KJV)*. The Bible is *a lamp unto my feet,* which means it shows me where I am. It is also a *light unto my path,* which means it shows me where I am going.

When we make God's Word a priority, we will read it regularly, and something most amazing will begin to happen; we will start to see ourselves in it. We will begin to see how we fit into God's plan. Preachers will read and find themselves connecting verses and making mental sermons. Intercessors will read and begin praying the promises of God down to earth. Worship

> No matter what your calling is, the Word will ignite it.

leaders will read and be inspired to sing about the glory of God as it is revealed to them. No matter what your calling is, the Word will ignite it. You are the light and the Word is like gasoline; when you come together, a spark will ignite. As the Holy Spirit makes the Word come alive, you will begin to see how you fit into God's kingdom.

It amazes me how one hundred ministries can have one hundred different visions. One ministry may focus on evangelism. One may focus on healing. Another may focus on mission work, while yet another feeds the poor. They are all following the same Spirit and reading the same Bible yet seeing it through different eyes, the eyes God has given them. The people leading these ministries were no doubt seeking the Lord and reading their Bibles when the Holy Spirit caused them to see themselves in the Word. Someone called to be a missionary is ignited by the verses about reaching out and serving. Someone with an evangelistic calling will be ignited by all the verses that talk about saving souls, and so on. Those who don't read the Bible never get ignited about anything! They don't discover what their uniqueness means to God. They remain lukewarm and ineffective and feel distant from God.

We are living in the information generation. There are so many resources available to those who want to learn about God. We have several different versions of the Bible, including the original Greek and Hebrew. We have concordances that can help us find any verse on any subject. There are thousands of websites that publish the Bible in every language. We can get the Bible on cassette tape, CD, DVD, or MP3. We can download it onto our IPods. We can read our Bible, listen to it in the car, or watch it on television with pictures. There is no excuse for this generation not to study the Bible!

Knowing God's Word is vital. We should not read it out of duty but because it is the source of our identity; it will reveal to us the hope of our calling. In it we will truly find freedom to be us.

CHAPTER 9:

BEING STILL

"Be still, and know that I am God…"

— *Psalm 46:10*

God's nature is gentle, patient, and longsuffering. God is not in a hurry, nor is He anxious. God is not moved in an instant, nor is He easily provoked. God is calm, cool and collected. The Bible teaches that *"with the Lord one day is like a thousand years, and a thousand years like one day" (2 Pet. 3:8)*. God is not pressured by deadlines or moved by time restraints. He's got it all figured out. We move around in this fast-paced world at lightning speed, missing God the whole way.

Proverbs 5:21 says, *"For the ways of man are before the eyes of the Lord, and He pondereth all his goings" (KJV)*. God is watching us zoom around in this fast food generation and He is pondering our goings. He desires us to slow down, talk to Him, and—better yet—listen to Him. We have created a world so fast-paced that we do not have time to be still. Even when we are sitting still we prefer the commotion of television or radio. We

> I jokingly say that everyone should spend their first year as a Christian in jail. I thank God for the many months I was forced to sit there in that jail—just me, God, and the King James Bible.

avoid silence and stillness, and by doing so we often avoid the presence of God.

One of the first things I learned to do as a new Christian was to *be still and know that He is God.* I was not taught to do this by man. In fact, anyone who knows me will probably testify that I am one of the most energetic (hyper) people they know. I have always been wide open; I do everything full throttle. For me it was a lot harder to sit still than it was to work. Perhaps this is why God did not save me until I was in jail! I had no choice but to *be still and know that He is God.*

Immediately after repenting of my sins, I began to just sit still and think about God. I would read some and then I would just sit there, totally quiet. This was a mighty principle which I learned by circumstance, and it paid dividends down the road. I jokingly say that everyone should spend their first year as a Christian in jail. I thank God for the many months I was forced to sit there in that jail—just me, God, and the King James Bible. It is one of the most difficult things for us humans to do: sit still. We would rather work and toil and move and make things happen; but God is not interested in what we can do. God is looking for those who will come to Him and be still in His presence.

I have heard people express how hard it is to hear from God, and often I ask "How much time do you spend listening to Him?" I already know the answer to the question; most of the time it is "little to none." We must remember that prayer is communication with God. Communication consists of speaking and **listening**. Most people who try to draw close to God sit down and start talking, shouting, and even crying. We sit down with a list and tell God everything that we want or need, or we just pray for everyone that we can think of and then say "amen." We walk away feeling almost exactly like we did before we started, with no answers, and then we say "God doesn't ever speak to me." What would happen if you got into the practice of going into a room, closing the door, and saying "God, I am here to listen to you"? I can tell you from experience that you would get answers to your problems and direction for your life.

We can get a clear picture of the stillness of God by reading about Elijah's escape from Jezebel in 1 Kings 19. Elijah had just killed four hundred of Jezebel's false prophets. So Jezebel had vowed to kill Elijah within twenty-four hours, as she did many other true prophets. Elijah ran for his life and ended up in a cave at Mount Horeb.

And he came thither unto a cave, and lodged there; and behold, the word of the Lord came to him, and he said unto him, What doest thou here, Elijah? And he said I have been very zealous for the Lord God of hosts: for the children of Israel have forsaken thy covenant, thrown down thine altars, and slain thy prophets with the sword; and I, even I only, am left; and they seek my life, to take it away. And he said, Go forth, and stand upon the mount before the Lord. And, behold, the Lord passed by, and a great and strong wind rent the mountains, and brake in pieces the rocks before the Lord; **but the Lord was not in the wind:** *and after the wind an earthquake;* **but the Lord was not in the earthquake.** *And after the earthquake a fire;* **but the Lord was not in the fire:** *and after the fire* **a still small voice.** *And it was so, when Elijah heard it, that he wrapped his face in his mantle, and went out, and stood in the entering in of the cave. And, behold, there came a voice unto him, and said, What doest thou here, Elijah? (1 Kings 19:9–13, KJV)*

THE SECRET PLACE

What a picture; God was not in the wind, the earthquake, or the fire; His presence was found in **stillness**. He speaks in a *still, small* voice. Elijah was not moved by any of the three earth-shaking events, but when he heard that familiar voice, he recognized it as God's and knew he'd better cover his face. One of the reasons we often can't hear from God is that we do not know how to quiet our soul; we have never learned how to *be still and know that He is God.* As previously discussed, in fellowship with God, He does not come down to our level but rather brings us up to His level, the level of the Spirit. We must be willing to leave the flesh realm if we want to enter the Spirit realm where God is. In the flesh realm we act carnal; we are guided by our emotions, which we display in a variety of ways. I have heard people shout at God to get His attention. I have been in very disturbing prayer meetings in which immature Christians act like two-year-old children throwing temper tantrums to get their way, rather than sons and daughters of God communicating with their Father.

Some think God will hear them better if they display emotion or act out; but my experience with the Lord is that He speaks only after we have quieted our souls and entered into the Spirit. This is sometimes a struggle. Let's face it, we all go through things every day that affect our emotions and make it difficult for us to quiet our souls. I have led prayer meetings in which we sit in silence for a period of time and just listen. It is interesting to watch people who are almost totally unable to just sit still and know that He is God. They fidget, squirm, and look at you as if to say "get on with it already!" These are often the same people who yell, shout, chant, and carry on in the flesh when it is their turn

> Some think God will hear them better if they display emotion or act out; but my experience with the Lord is that He speaks only after we have quieted our souls.

to pray. I call this "emotionalism," and I have found that God does not respond to it.

If we want to really hear from God and fellowship with Him, we must learn to daily shut down our flesh and make it submit to the Spirit. Shutting down our flesh means not allowing our feelings and emotions to move our actions. It means giving our spirit man the control. It is like telling our flesh to "shut up!" Doing this is paramount if we desire fellowship with God. By routinely shutting down our flesh, we develop sensitivity to God's voice. We become aware of His presence. We lose sight of ourselves and begin to see the Lord. God's Spirit will minister to our spirit when our flesh is taken out of the way.

Remember that Jesus said, *"It is the Spirit who gives life; **the flesh profits nothing"** (John 6:63)*. In other words, as long as you are controlled by your flesh, you will not get anywhere. Romans 8:8 says, *"So then they that are in the flesh cannot please God" (KJV)*. It is the Spirit that we are after, because it is He who gives life. We must get in the practice of quieting our soul before God!

Let me make this very practical and easy to apply; I am telling you to learn to get alone with the Lord and *do nothing!* Just listen. When you feel like you have to **do** something like talk, yell, pace, cry or any of the many acts we do to display our emotions—refuse. Refuse to allow your flesh to take you out of the quiet stillness that is displayed in God's character. There is a time to talk, yell, pace, cry, and show emotion. This seems easy for us to do; but we must not neglect the time when we are to be still and quiet, waiting upon the Lord.

CHAPTER 10:

WAITING ON THE LORD

The next principle is a spinoff of the last. Once we learn to be still and know that He is God, we must also learn to **wait upon the Lord**. Isaiah 40:30–31 says, *"Even the youths shall faint and be weary, and the young men shall utterly fall: But they that **wait upon the Lord** shall renew their strength; they shall mount up with wings as eagles; they shall run, and not be weary; and they shall walk, and not faint" (KJV).*

There is a key principle in this verse: those who *wait* upon the Lord will *renew* their strength. Did you know that your strength must be *renewed?* When our strength is not renewed, we become weary and weak, and we may even fall. We cannot run this week on last week's strength. We cannot fight tomorrow's battle with today's strength. A lot of Christians are weary and weak all of the time; they live in defeat and confusion because they have no strength. How can this be? We have not learned to *wait upon the Lord.* It is one thing to quiet your soul; it is another to *wait upon the Lord.* True strength flows from God to us as we *wait.* It is like going to the gas station to refuel.

The Hebrew word for *wait upon* is Qawah; it means "to bind together, to be joined; to lie in wait for someone; to expect; to await; to trust in." This is a powerful truth. We must get quiet before the Lord so that we can *wait upon Him*, so we can be joined to Him, Spirit to spirit. This is why we were saved: to be reconciled to God. As we *wait* on Him, we will be bound together with Him; this is intimacy with God. It is not about how long you are a Christian, what denomination you belong to, how much education you have, or how much money you have in the bank. The secrets to intimacy with God are *being still and knowing that He is God* and *waiting upon Him to renew our strength*. This is so easy a child could do it. You do not have to be smart to have fellowship with God; some actually need to lose all of their smarts and learn to be totally dependent on God. Some of us run around all day in the flesh, making emotional decisions, and then spend three minutes at night asking God to bless what we did before saying amen. Then we run off and do it again the next day.

This will never get us closer to fulfilling the purposes of God for our lives. This causes us to suffer stress and anxiety; it keeps us feeling lost and confused about our purpose. We may go to church, but we feel out of place; we feel like there is more to life; we long to really experience God. I hope some of you who are reading this realize that I am describing your life. I hope you understand the error of your ways. But most of all, I hope you understand that God is looking to draw near to you. Forget your failures and come to God with a childlike faith that says, "Teach me, Lord, to have intimacy with You." God is looking for such; He longs for fellowship with His children. He has plans for your life that will never be accomplished until you draw near to Him. There are things that He wants to teach you, things that are only for you. Will you sit and listen?

Waiting on God will go against everything that your flesh wants. The flesh is all about the "doing," but we must be all about the "waiting." Before you try this, let me warn you; it may seem like nothing is happening and you are totally wasting your time. You may want to get up and give up, but if you persevere and make a practice of giving God the time to draw near to you, you will have a breakthrough.

No one knew the power of waiting on the Lord quite like king David, who wrote about it often in his psalms. Here are a few that show how important this principle was to him:

Lead me in thy truth, and teach me: for thou art the God of my salvation; on thee do I wait all the day (Ps. 25:5, KJV).

Wait on the Lord: be of good courage, and he shall strengthen thine heart: wait, I say, on the Lord (Ps. 27:14, KJV).

Rest in the Lord, and wait patiently for him: fret not thyself because of him who prospereth in his way, because of the man who bringeth wicked devices to pass. Cease from anger, and forsake wrath: fret not thyself in any wise to do evil. For evildoers shall be cut off: but those that wait upon the Lord, they shall inherit the earth (Ps. 37:7–9, KJV).

My soul waiteth for the Lord more than they that watch for the morning: I say, more than they that watch for the morning (Ps. 130:6, KJV).

Let not them that wait on thee, O Lord GOD of hosts, be ashamed for my sake (Ps. 69:6, KJV).

There are many, many more passages like these, but I believe these prove the scriptural strength of this principle.

The American church at large has neglected the principle of waiting. We have become seeker friendly. In some cases, we are breeding ignorant followers of a watered down religion. This is catastrophic! We must be the people that God has called us to be, or else why would anyone want what we have? It is like there is an unspoken rule dictating that we should all pretend we walk in fellowship with God, whether we do or not. Closeness to God is not something you can fake for very long. Pretty soon your life will have to clearly show some fruit. In other words, people should be able to see in you a blessed life of purpose and power. Then they will want what you have; they will covet your Jesus.

Besides renewing my strength, there is another thing that waiting on the Lord has done for me personally. It happened around the third year that I walked with God. All of a sudden I developed a *new confidence and trust* in the Lord. I became much more confident that He was with me and would meet me when I sought Him. I felt I could go to Him at any time and hear from Him. Suddenly I was walking in full assurance that I was with Him and that His hand was upon everything I did. This verse came alive to me: *"For in him we live, and move, and have our being"* *(Acts 17:28, KJV)*. I went beyond merely acknowledging the doctrine that God never leaves us; I began to live with a strong inner confidence that God was always with *me*. I became very bold. I no longer needed approval from man; I had gained the approval of my Father. That feeling sustains me even to this day. I am talking about knowing who you are and where you stand with God. I am talking about going beyond just hoping you have been accepted by God. It is possible to walk in confident boldness with Him. You can reach this level of assurance over time by learning to wait upon Him. As you consistently wait upon Him, He will consistently renew your strength. Eventually, you will live in the continual strength that is available only in the Secret Place of God.

Just look at the lives of Moses, Joshua, David, Elijah, Elisha, Joseph, Peter, Paul and many other men who were connected to God. They were marked by strength. They were marked by boldness and confidence in the Lord. I believe that we can all walk in that kind of assurance, if we learn to *wait upon the Lord.*

CHAPTER 11:

PERSEVERANCE

Throughout my ministry I have discipled many new Christians, teaching them all the importance of living holy, obedient lives by surrender to Jesus. I have watched many come to Jesus full of excitement and anticipation of their new life with Him. And then it happens. They crash into the reality of what they have committed to, the reality of forsaking sinful practice, the reality of cross-bearing self denial. This is when it gets tough. When all the goose bumps are gone and all the "high fives" are finished, they have to *work out their salvation* (Phil. 2:12). They have to follow through. Many give up there, and it breaks my heart to see it happen. I want to let them have a piece of the satisfaction I feel every day from knowing I am accepted by God, but I can't. What they need is the last key principle that I want to give: **perseverance.**

If I had to give one word that I felt would totally revive today's lukewarm church, it would be "perseverance." I am not talking about just "hanging on." I am talking about pressing in and pressing on with a vigilant attitude that won't take no for an answer. Perseverance is not just settling for "ok." It is a drive for the divine, abundant life found in Christ.

We start off with this drive, but how long does it last? Some of you pastors and evangelists know what I am talking about. You have watched painfully as many have turned back to their old lives; they could not pay the price. "Why," we ask ourselves. "Why would they choose to go back to that old life without Jesus?" The answer in almost every case is a lack of perseverance. We all want to be successful, anointed, blessed, joyous and victorious Christians, but we do not want to pay the price for it. We want fellowship with God; we want to feel close and hear His voice, but are we willing to persevere to get it? We must purpose in our hearts to make fellowship with God a reality in our lives; we can't take no for an answer. We need bold faith; we need perseverance. We must believe God's Word and hold Him to it. We must proceed with confidence in what His Word promises.

I believe one reason that many people fail spiritually is that no one prepares them to stand up to the difficulty they will face almost immediately after deciding to follow Jesus. We sell people on the idea that being a Christian is simple. We tell them how much satisfaction we get from knowing the Lord. We talk about the blessings and joy and peace, but what about the hardships, the pressure of the battle, and the difficulties involved? In some cases, we present only the benefits of

> In our zeal to make converts, we have neglected an important principle: counting the cost.

Christianity while we avoid the challenges. This has led to a lot of incomplete conversions and a great falling away in the body of Christ. In our zeal to make converts, we have neglected an important principle: **counting the cost**.

Luke 14:28 says, *"For which of you, intending to build a tower, sitteth not down first, and **counteth the cost,** whether he have sufficient to finish it?" (KJV)* Jesus presented this question while teaching about becoming His disciple. It is important for each person to sit down **first** to count the cost, to see if he or she is willing to pay the price.

To do this, one must first know what the price is. In the same chapter, Jesus explained the price of being His disciple: *"So likewise, whosoever he be of you that forsaketh not all that he hath, he cannot be my disciple" (Luke 14:33, KJV)*. Jesus said we must "forsake all that we have" to be His disciples. The cost of following Jesus is the willingness to lay down all that is not of God. If we do not say yes to that price before we begin to build our new life in Christ, it will ultimately end in failure and frustration.

One reason that more "average" believers are not experiencing this closeness or "fellowship" with the Lord is that, years after their salvation, they are still counting the cost. They have never really begun building. Building cannot begin until one agrees to pay the price. It is essential to our spiritual growth to sit down **first** and count the cost. Once we settle this, we must be ready to write the check. We must expect difficulty and hardship.

Peter said, *"Think it not strange concerning the fiery trial which is to try you, as though some strange thing happened unto you" (1 Peter 4:12, KJV)*. It is not unusual for new believers to be thrust into **fiery trials**. It is kingdom protocol. We must go in with an attitude that says, "I will persevere. I will maintain my confidence!"

Hebrews 10:35 says, *"Therefore, do not throw away your **confidence**, which has a great reward."* A person who loses confidence in the promise of God should never look for a reward. We can never draw near to God with doubt and pessimism. God's Word tells us to *"draw near with a sincere heart in full assurance of faith" (Heb. 10:22)*. It is time that we enter His presence and show Him our sincerity by believing His Word. We cannot come with the attitude that says, "Well, I guess I will give it a try." We can't say "I hope this works." We must be confident that what the Lord has promised will *surely* come to pass. The Lord finds pleasure in our confidence and assurance of His promises.

> *Do not throw away your confidence, which has a great reward. For you have need of **endurance**, so that when you have done the will of God, you may receive what was promised. For yet in a very little while, he who is coming will come and will not delay. But my righteous one shall live by faith; and if he shrinks back, my soul has no pleasure in him (Heb. 10:35–38).*

How many souls have been on the verge of breakthrough when they have given up? Many come close to receiving the promise but draw back prematurely due to doubt, unbelief, frustration and confusion. These feelings *will* attempt to overtake our confidence, but we must not allow them to!

Every good thing in life costs something. Anything worth something is worth fighting for. In Jude 1:3 we are encouraged to "*earnestly contend* for the faith which was once delivered unto the saints" (KJV). We are called to "*fight the good fight* of faith" in 1 Timothy 6:12; "*war a good warfare*" in 1 Timothy 1:18(KJV); and "*endure hardness, as a good soldier*" in 2 Timothy 2:3 (KJV). There is a sort of theme in the Bible: we are not called to simply enjoy our stay on earth; the call of the Christian is a call to battle. It is so important for us to learn how to contend for the faith. God *will* show up. He *will* draw near to us; but we must come to Him in confidence. We must wait on Him with endurance and refuse to shrink back into unbelief and frustration. We must persevere to receive the promises of the Secret Place of the Most High.

> We are not called to simply enjoy our stay on earth; the call of the Christian is a call to battle.

CHAPTER 12:

THE FELLOWSHIP OF HIS SUFFERINGS

"That I may know Him and the power of His resurrection and the fellowship of His sufferings, being conformed to His death."

— *Philippians 3:10*

It was Paul's prayer to know Jesus. More specifically, his prayer was to know Jesus in the capacity or in the "fellowship" of His sufferings. What a bold request! We seem to look for fellowship with Christ in blessing, victory, joy and good times, but what about the fellowship of His sufferings?

The call of the Christian is a call to suffer. When I use the word "suffering," I am talking about hardship, grief, discomfort, and mental and emotional turmoil. It is when all hell seems to break loose. It is when you do everything right and things still go wrong. It is the fellowship of **Christ's** sufferings. Jesus did everything right. He suffered not because of His faults but for ours. When we suffer for the cause of Christ, we are partaking of **His** sufferings.

As Christ's followers, we are automatically called to this. Think about the commands of Jesus; He said, *"Love your enemies, do good to those who hate you, bless those who curse you, pray for those who mistreat you" (Luke 6:27–28).* He taught us to go the extra mile. If someone slaps your right cheek you are to offer them the left also. To obey these commands, one must *choose* to suffer.

Jesus was betrayed by His friend, denied by His disciple, and blasphemed by many. He was beaten without a cause, mocked by His own creation, tortured by evil men, and killed for our iniquity. He suffered for *us.* He left us an example of how we too should suffer.

Paul understood this principle and welcomed the sufferings and hardships of Christ. I don't get the impression from Paul's writings that he prayed much for blessings or good times. Paul knew the heartbeat of Christ and truly chose to suffer and endure hardship for Jesus' name.

You may be wondering why this is relevant. You may be asking what the fellowship of His sufferings has to do with the Secret Place. It is important because the sufferings of Christ hold a special place in the heart of God. God had to watch His Son endure ridicule, shame and torture. God watched His Son maintain His composure while being lied about. He watched as every possible comfort was stripped away from Jesus. God, like any proud Father, watched His Son overcome adversity and remain faithful, and it brought Him pleasure.

There is a part of the heart of God that carries the memory of Christ's sufferings. When God sees us choose to suffer for Jesus by maintaining our composure in the midst of adversity, it brings Him pleasure. Every day we are put in situations that test or stretch us. We are treated wrongly, pushed past our limit, lied about, or falsely accused. When we maintain a Christlike attitude in the midst of that, the Father finds pleasure.

THE SECRET PLACE

Suffering for Christ touches the heart of God. Look at the early church. Acts 6 and 7 tell us about Stephen, who was chosen to serve food to widows. It was a time of tremendous persecution, but Stephen fearlessly proclaimed the Gospel throughout the city. When he was brought before the council, they lied about him and wrongly accused him. He boldly witnessed to them about the power of Jesus Christ, and they stoned him to death. As they were killing him, heaven opened up and he saw Jesus standing at the right hand of God, ready to receive him into heaven.

Another example is that of Moses, who was raised as a prince in Egypt. Hebrews 11:24–26 says,

By faith Moses, when he had grown up, refused to be called the son of Pharaoh's daughter, choosing rather to endure ill-treatment with the people of God than to enjoy the passing pleasures of sin, considering the reproach of Christ greater riches than the treasures of Egypt.

Moses refused to live for pleasure. He embraced suffering, and as a result God used him to rescue Israel from slavery.

Look at the men of the Bible who had the closest relationships with God, the men who walked in the greatest power. You will see a common theme; they all suffered hardship. Daniel was thrown to lions, David was betrayed by many, Elijah was hunted by Jezebel, and Jeremiah was thrown in the dungeon. Joseph was sold into slavery; Paul, Peter, and John were put in prison; James was killed with the sword; Stephen was stoned; and Jesus was crucified.

We have a misconception that the Christian life should be smooth sailing. I have heard one too many sermons on how easy being a Christian is. If your Christian life is so easy and trouble free, I wonder how fruitful it has been. We can choose to suffer hardship and embrace discomfort, or we can avoid it and take the easy way. Anyone who chooses the path to closeness with God can expect suffering along the way. As the Word says, *"Yea, and **all** that will live **godly** in Christ Jesus shall suffer persecution" (2 Tim. 3:12, KJV).*

When you say yes to the fellowship of Christ's sufferings, something powerful happens. You partner with Jesus in the reconciliation of man to God. *"For God so loved the world, that He gave His only begotten Son" (John 3:16).* If there is any question about what motivates God, it is answered in that He gave up His only Son to suffer for the purpose of reconciling the world to Himself.

> *And all things are of God, who hath reconciled us to himself by Jesus Christ, and hath given to us the ministry of reconciliation; To wit, that God was in Christ, reconciling the world unto himself, not imputing their trespasses unto them; and hath committed unto us the word of reconciliation (2 Cor. 5:18–19, KJV).*

We have all been given the same ministry; it is the "ministry of reconciliation." How did Jesus reconcile man to God? He did it through His bloodshed; He did it through suffering. The Bible says that *"Jesus Christ is the same yesterday and today and forever" (Heb. 13:8).* Jesus is still active. The Jesus who died to save still lives to reconcile God and man. In order to get close to Him, you must be where He is. When we partake of His sufferings, when we choose to leave our comfort zones and be stretched, closeness with the Lord will surely follow.

> When you say yes to the fellowship of Christ's sufferings, you partner with Jesus in the reconciliation of man to God.

We develop closeness with Him not by merely going to church or praying before meals, but by getting involved in His ministry. We must

69

be ready to get our hands dirty. It is when you feel His pain, denial, betrayal, hardship, and frustration that you partake of His sufferings.

Sometimes avoiding hardship means avoiding fellowship with Christ. The Holy Spirit may lead us into difficult situations. It was the Holy Spirit who "drove" Jesus into the wilderness to be tempted (Mark 1:12–13). What if the fulfillment of God's plan requires that you suffer hardship? Will you avoid or embrace it?

Some might say "God does not want us to suffer." But the Bible teaches the contrary. Here are some examples:

*For it is better, if the will of God be so, that you **suffer for well doing,** than for evil doing (1 Pet. 3:17, KJV).*

*Wherefore let them that **suffer according to the will of God** commit the keeping of their souls to him in well doing, as unto a faithful Creator (1Pet. 4:19, KJV).*

*But the God of all grace, who hath called us unto his eternal glory by Christ Jesus, **after that ye have suffered a while,** make you perfect, establish, strengthen, settle you (1Pet. 5:10, KJV).*

*If we **suffer,** we shall also reign with him: if we deny him, he also will deny us (2 Tim. 2:12, KJV).*

There are many more verses that clearly declare that Christians should expect to suffer for Christ. Why, then, do we have this idea in America that our Christian experience should be easy and problem free? This thinking has made it hard for the average, assuming, and misled believer to experience a close relationship with the Lord.

I want to encourage those who might have experienced the fellowship of Christ's sufferings and responded improperly.

Maybe you were wrongly accused and instead of enduring it you lashed out and responded in an ungodly way. Maybe you have crumbled under the pressure of persecution and it has led you into depression and regret. I encourage you to stand up, confess it to God, and soften your heart. I encourage you to forgive your enemies and pray for those who have spitefully used you. As Jesus said of those who were killing Him, *"Father, forgive them; for they do not know what they are doing" (Luke 23:34).*

Realistically, we can expect to be used and abused by someone at some time; but we cannot let these experiences shape our attitudes or defile our character.

It is sometimes easy to get offended and hurt in church. I write this as one who has experienced a dramatic, ungodly encounter in church. I was on the leadership team in a church for about one year. The church's direction seemed to change; some of the leaders got wrapped up in teaching things that they found on the Internet that seemed "spiritual" instead of personally seeking words from the Lord. I felt that the emphasis had shifted from saving and discipling souls to angelic visitations, miracles, signs, and wonders. Feeling like things were getting out of focus, I addressed my concerns to others in leadership. Within a few months, two of the other leaders began to talk negatively about me to others behind my back. Lies were told about me; secret meetings were held. Things I had said were taken out of context and twisted. Eventually, I was actually kicked out of the church. My wife and I were hurt badly.

At first I wanted to fight back; I wanted to stick up for myself and show people the truth. I was angry and hurt by the ones I had called my friends. For several days I fumed about how I would have handled the situation. I wanted truth to prevail! I prayed and asked God what I should do. The Lord reminded me of something that had happened many weeks before. I had been studying about the fellowship of Christ's sufferings. I was moved one Sunday in church to go to the altar. I prayed "Lord, I want to partake of your sufferings." I heard the Lord respond to me, "Do you know what you are asking Me?" I thought about it for a moment before saying, "Yes, Lord, I know. I want to partake of Your sufferings."

Many weeks went by. I forgot almost totally about that prayer and went on to something different. Then the sufferings of Christ took me by surprise and I was devastated. I got just a small taste of what it feels like to be rejected, falsely accused and misunderstood. That feeling was almost more than I could bear; I was ready to respond in my flesh.

I repented and asked God to help me forgive. I called my mentor, Francis, and told him about it. He told me I should write a letter thanking them for releasing me from the church; then I should move on. I did it, and after many months I was able to totally move on mentally and walk in forgiveness. Within a year, that church closed down. The last I heard, a small group of them changed the name of the church and now hold meetings in a home. I pray for them to this day.

The lesson I learned was priceless. We are sometimes made to suffer wrongly, but those situations are opportunities to actually feel the frustration of Christ, to literally partake of **His** suffering. If you want to experience the Secret Place of the Most High, you must also embrace the fellowship of Christ's sufferings, as the two are divinely connected.

CHAPTER 13:

THE UNION

I want to describe what I think is the grand climax of Christianity. The great event that all believers are destined for is a *marriage*. More specifically, it is our marriage to Jesus. This is clear from the parable of the wedding banquet in Matthew 22:2–14. It starts by saying, *"The kingdom of heaven may be compared to a king (God) who gave a wedding feast for his son (Jesus)."*

We are called to be the "bride" of Christ. Without getting all weird, this means that we are called to be in total fellowship with the Lord in such a way that we become *one*. This is what happens in marriage. Ephesians 5:31 says, *"For this reason a man shall leave his father and mother and shall be joined to his wife, **and the two shall become one flesh.**"* The next verse applies the same principle to our union with Christ: *"This mystery is great; but I am speaking with reference to Christ and the church."*

What a mystery: two separate entities becoming so intertwined that you can't tell where one ends and the other begins. This is the mystery of our relationship to God through Jesus Christ. Now, I know that most do not possess this level of devotion and fellowship with Christ, but it is what we are called to. Jesus expressed this in His prayer in John 17, the night before He would go to the cross. He addressed His followers, telling them that it was His time to be crucified. He prayed for His disciples that God would keep them from evil and guard them. Then He said,

> *I do not ask on behalf of these alone,* **but for those also who believe in Me through their word; that they may all be one; even as You, Father, are in Me and I in You, that they also may be in Us,** *so that the world may believe that you sent Me. The glory which you have given Me I have given to them,* **that they may be one, just as We are one** *(John 17:20–22).*

In this prayer Jesus included everyone who would come to Him through His disciples' words. Think about that; Jesus was praying for *you and me* before He went to the cross. Do you believe Jesus' prayer will be answered? I do. And what was His prayer? That we may be one with Jesus and the Father in the same way that Jesus was one with the Father.

We often have too narrow a view for our Christian walk. It is a marriage to God through Jesus that we are after, and this goes beyond regular church attendance. It is Jesus' prayer that we would share the same fellowship with God that He did while He was on earth.

> Jesus was praying for you and me before He went to the cross. Do you believe Jesus' prayer will be answered?

While on earth, Jesus constantly ventured off to pray and have fellowship alone with God. He was going to His Secret Place to draw near to His Father. It is the perfect picture; Jesus walked with God all day, but at certain times He would stop everything He was doing and spend one-on-one time with His Father. It was Jesus' priority to have fellowship with God. Sometimes He would spend all night in this fellowship, not even stopping to sleep! Let's look at the outcome of Jesus' secret relationship with God. John 5:19 says,

> *Therefore Jesus answered and was saying to them, "Truly, truly, I say to you, the Son can do nothing of Himself, unless it is something He sees the Father doing; for whatever the Father does, these things the Son also does in like manner."*

Jesus did not just stumble around healing people and preaching. He walked precisely and purposefully, doing only what He saw the Father do. He spent time every day with God to find out what He should do, and then He did it. Jesus' fellowship with God shook the entire region and eventually the entire world for generations to come, and it is still shaking the world today. When the ministry of Jesus on earth was complete, His disciples carried it through until now by learning to abide in the same fellowship with the Father that Jesus did. They were all world changers; they were forces to be reckoned with.

What would happen if the entire body of Christ entered into this type of fellowship with God? What would happen in your family, life, and church if you entered into devoted, daily fellowship with God? You too would become a world changer. God is not done working in the world; He is still looking for willing vessels to be used to shake the earth as witnesses of Jesus Christ.

The Lord is looking for a bride, someone He can unite with and fulfill His purposes through. What an honor—an honor He has made available to "whosoever will."

CHAPTER 14:

MAKING READY

"If anyone is thirsty, let him come to Me and drink."

— *John 7:37*

There is a river that flows from God. There is a place of satisfaction. There is abundant life available to those who desire it. You can taste heaven while living on earth!

There is a river whose streams make glad the city of God, the holy dwelling places of the Most High. God is in the midst of her, she will not be moved; God will help her when morning dawns (Ps. 46:4–5).

We can be saturated with the presence of the Lord. I want to encourage you to reposition yourself. Put yourself in position to experience the Lord in a new and fresh way. God desires to develop you and bring you to the knowledge of who you are in Him. It is the Lord's desire that you know your calling and place in His kingdom. God is looking for His children to get serious about their relationship with Him. It is clear from the Bible that the days leading up to His return will be action-packed. The Lord plans to accomplish many things before the Rapture.

He will use His church to fulfill all that He has predetermined. Just think—God has planned to do big things through *you*.

What an exciting day we are living in. In the midst of economic difficulty, wars and rumors of wars all over the world, God is still in control. God still runs everything; nothing happens outside of His will. As the Word teaches, not one sparrow falls to the ground apart from the will of God (Matt. 10:29). And two verses later Jesus said, *"Fear ye not therefore, ye are of more value than many sparrows" (KJV)*. You are valuable to God. The Lord has something invested in you; He has an interest in you. God wants you to find your destiny.

"Let us be glad and rejoice, and give honour to him: for the marriage of the Lamb is come, and his wife hath made herself ready" (Rev. 19:7, KJV). This verse was spoken by a voice that John heard coming out of heaven during the vision he recorded in the book of Revelation. John said that the voice was of a great multitude which sounded like "many waters" (Rev. 19:6). It is obvious that this voice was declaring the return of Jesus Christ for His marriage to us (His church). Heaven waits with expectation to herald the long awaited day when Jesus claims His bride.

What catches my attention is the part that says *"And his wife hath made herself ready."* The bride of Christ will be a body of His followers who have made up their mind to prepare for His coming. A lot of preparations go into a wedding. The bride spends countless hours making sure that everything is perfect. She will undoubtedly ensure that she presents herself to her bridegroom looking the absolute best that she can. How much more should we prepare to meet our King?

> A lot of preparations go into a wedding... How much more should we prepare to meet our King?

THE SECRET PLACE

There is a cry from heaven for us to make ready. The Lord is summoning His bride. He is calling us to come closer to Him. He is calling us to put on our wedding garment and position ourselves for a marriage-like relationship with Him.

Never has the parable of the ten virgins (Matt. 25:1–13) been so relevant. In this parable Jesus compared the kingdom of heaven to ten virgins (believers) who went to meet the bridegroom (Jesus). The Bible says that five of them were wise and five were foolish. The foolish took their lamps but took no oil with them. The wise took their lamps and also brought oil. Matthew 25:5–13 says,

> *While the bridegroom tarried, they all slumbered and slept. And at midnight there was a cry made, Behold, the bridegroom cometh: go ye out to meet him. Then all those virgins arose, and trimmed their lamps. And the foolish said unto the wise, Give us of your oil; for our lamps are gone out. But the wise answered, saying, Not so: lest there be not enough for us and you: but go ye rather to them that sell, and buy for yourselves. And while they went to buy, the bridegroom came;* **and they that were ready went in with him to the marriage:** *and the door was shut. Afterward came also the other virgins, saying, Lord, Lord, open to us. But he answered and said, Verily I say unto you, I know you not. Watch therefore, for you know neither the day nor the hour wherein the Son of man cometh (KJV).*

The Lord came at an inopportune time. He came at the midnight hour, a time of darkness. There was no time to prepare for the marriage. Again it is noted here that *they that were ready went in with him to the marriage.* We must prepare while there is still light. Jesus said,

> *Yet a little while is the light with you. Walk while you have the light, lest darkness come upon you: for he that walketh in darkness knoweth not whither he goeth (John 12:35, KJV).*

Wherever in your journey this book finds you, I encourage you to move forward. You can have fellowship with God; you can be close to Jesus. I will end with this verse, heaven's plea:

And the Spirit and the bride say, Come. And let him that heareth say, Come. And let him that is athirst come. And whosoever will, let him take the water of life freely (Rev 22:17, KJV).

God Bless!

Erin James Sain